The Transmigrate Manifesto

Keegan Beekman

Published by The Owl of Freedom, 2024.

THE TRANSMIGRATE MANIFESTO

First edition. July 30, 2024.

Copyright © 2024 Keegan Beekman.

ISBN: 979-8227672124

Written by Keegan Beekman.

Table of Contents

I envision a world where we do not care what skin color, dialect, religion or region one comes from. I envision a world where your love for your fellow man drives you to help one another, drives you to contribute in society any way you feel fit, and directs you to think of solutions to problems. I envision a world where we are not repressed, and a world with neither war nor struggle due to lack. I envision a world where people can do what they please without being discriminated against. I envision a world where there is no worry about buying necessities, or not getting proper nutrition or healthcare. I envision a world that is truly free for all who live on this planet: the plants, the animals, the children, the elderly who cannot seem to get the care they need to retire or the care of professionals, including the beings who do not dwell on the surface of our planet. I believe that all it requires is for one person to stand up to the world powers, and say enough is enough; we are tired of the false narratives of separation and war, we are tired of slave labor just to make ends meet, we are tired of what the governments are doing to other people, and most of all, we are tired of the imposed fear. I believe all it takes is for one person to spark a revolution. I believe all it takes is for one person to stand fully in their power to spark the flame of making the world truly free of tyranny.

Yes, there will be problems that will arise, there may still be some bloodshed in the defense of our new nation, and of course, it will take everyone banding together, but enough is enough. Now is the time for true freedom. If the past few years have taught us anything and the next ones don't reinforce it, it is that the government believes they are invincible, and nothing bad can be done against them, but they truly fear and see their system of control being pulled from underneath their feet. All it takes is for us to study the January 6th insurrection to understand that the politicians really fear what the people are capable of doing. It was such a minor event compared to the riots that were instilled by the higher ups with the Black Lives Matter movement, but these politicians were not the ones living through it, so when these riots come to their doorstep they curl up into a little ball and proclaim it is the worst thing ever. The controllers, even at the lower levels, fear what we the people can do, so we must act soon before our liberties are stripped away from us, before we cannot take a stand, and before our minds and the media are controlled to the point of no return. We as a civilization must realize the injustices done against us and do something about them. I neither claim to know what the perfect steps are, nor do I claim to be the bearer of freedom alone, but it is my belief that if you free your mind and soul, you will live a life truly free of tyranny.

- Keegan Beekman

Authors Note and Purpose of the Manifesto

This work was completed at the end of February 2024, I have not updated any information even as some of it came true such as the Hawaii wildfire story. The purpose of these warnings is so that they can be stopped, unfortunately for Hawaii billionaires already bought the land are actively working on the 15 minute cities like I warned. The only information I added since February is additional information about the pearl harbor part, general editing for sentences that didn't sound quite right, and the inclusion of a sneak peak of Novi Popul Ordinis. Novi Popul Ordinis is going to end up being a large book, I just hope is not too late when it is finally finished.

In this material, you are encouraged to swallow your pride and look at the bigger picture, no matter how you feel. By doing that, you will read many things that you may not enjoy but is necessary to understand what is going on in the current society and discover ways we can alter the situation. I say the things that need to be said without regard to feelings in this material. I also share knowledge that is not normally privy to most, and if you take nothing else from this, I hope I would have opened your mind up to further possibilities of said material. There are obviously more problems in this world than I can physically know or write about, so I will try to touch on the major issues and offer possible solutions to them. This is designed to be [a] point of discussion, and I urge anyone reading this material [to] share and discuss it, as well as add to and/or ratify the materi[al.] There has never been a problem that has been solved with t[he] same level of consciousness that created it, so discuss th[is] material with love for each other. None of what I say is mea[nt] to hurt anyone without a just cause, so don't be the person wh[o] tries to impose what is right and wrong unto another fellow ma[n,] because I don't think you are the one that decides what is rig[ht] and wrong. This is unless you are the one being imposed on [by] someone else who is telling you what is right from wrong; in th[at] case, act accordingly and investigate the situation.

I don't want this important information to be complicate[d] for two reasons: one reason is to get this information out as soo[n] as possible, and secondly, I want people to do their own researc[h] on the subjects involved, most of which will require more tha[n] a simple Google search to find the answers. It will require th[e] willingness to dig deeper into not only what the government [is] doing to the people, but what the hidden powers are doing to th[e] people.

Once I finish writing this short-winded version, I wi[ll] immediately begin to work on the full version, where I wi[ll] explain the things I know about certain subjects, withou[t] worrying about what the reader will think about these subjects. [I] want the reader to make their own informed opinion about wha[t] I talk about before I explain unfamiliar topics that may shatte[r] their view on the world and religion. I also will add a great dea[l] to the *Changes to the Government* chapter and *The Hypocris[y] of Our Controllers* chapter. I will have something special don[e] for *The Declaration of Independence* chapter; there will also b[e] an addition of extra sections. All these sections will be greatly expanded upon with additional information and ideas.

In the process of writing this Manifesto, I have been followed by private investigators, had my car's electronics turned off on top of a bridge in the rain, had my phone tapped, and attacked in other ways that I won't mention until I release the extended version. The controllers of our world wish to keep the status quo of freedom and will do anything to stop the impending rebellion of the people, be it peacefully or aggressively. I do not fear for my life the way others do, nor do I fear the government taking my life, for they know the true nature of a soul, which I will not mention here due to credibility reasons. However, in the extended cut I will leave nothing unearthed. I do not wish to hide from the people I am meant to inspire for I have no quarrel with death; I must shine the light in the darkest places no matter the cost.

With that being said, if you do not have a great deal of time to read this Manifesto, the main points of discussion are the depopulation agenda, the control agenda — which are one of the same — how the system is failing us, and how we can change that. If you have a little bit of time, I recommend you read the Declaration of Independence section, as there is a mirroring of the tyranny the British were imposing on our founding fathers, and the tyranny the government is imposing on us today. This is merely a point being made in this version and it is not what I envision the section to be in the full Manifesto. I put forth ideas on how we can grow past our current system, which is not by simply destroying it in its entirety, but by taking the good parts and getting rid of the bad parts, focusing on freedom for everyone. As we continue to yearn for more freedom, we shall have stops in place to work on our newfound government, or we may decide we don't need most of it anymore. Now, we may feel the government we have made is fit for our protection, but I feel that if we decide to have a one world government, we may need to workshop it again, however, time will tell.

The Current State of Democracy

" *He who has eyes to see, let him see, and he who has ears to hear, let him hear."*

- Matthew 13:9-16

Although many people find comfort living in a country or an area for generations, these dispositions must be set aside when that comfortable living is repeatedly stripped away by the ones who lit and passed the torch not only to us, but our ancestors.

I know I must not sit idle any longer as society quickly becomes more constricting, especially these past few years. The governments of the world seek to harm people physically and emotionally by any means possible, and even ways you think they cannot. The people are starting to wake up to realize the government is consistently failing us but the media portrays it as nonsense. We are all slaves to the system but we must realize we don't need to be. All it takes is for one person to stand up with a viable solution and say enough is enough. If what they say truly is a viable solution, people will follow him/her, but the problem is most people want to rework the system to accommodate the people of today, and the truth is, it cannot be reworked. Realistically, most people in the population are in the lower-class, with the middle-class being millionaires, and the upper-class being billionaires, or near so. As the wage gap increases and the lower-class continues to worsen, there is a need for help. At the moment, I do not see the government collapsing as some might suggest, but a great deal of changes still need to take place. Other countries question what is really going on in the States, but of course, they too are under total control as well and have equal, if not worse problems in some ways.

Why are we seen by other countries as fat, lazy, and oddly enough, workaholics? Why is there a huge discrepancy in the information? Personally, I would attribute it to propaganda, not only in other countries but ours as well. It doesn't take a rocket scientist to realize that when you go to a store, the majority of the people should not be overweight. I do not mean to ruffle anyone's feathers with me saying that, but it's the truth. Interestingly, it really isn't your fault, as the food industries are actively feeding us poison in everything we consume, and we are also choosing to consume these items, knowing they contain more calories, fat or sugars which are bad for our health, but that really isn't the true story behind most of what we consume. The worst part of this is that the government actively knows these are poisons and yet, they do nothing to really inform the public on the dangers of these poisons. In fact, they encourage us to eat some of these poisons. A lot of the time, when information comes out on these items, it's brushed off, or it's banned for consumption, but they don't ban it for other purposes, so it will eventually find its way into the food we eat, such as the case with certain chemicals used in farming. The same goes for medicine; the government will actively approve medicine that kills people, or has an extreme number of side effects, as well as hidden substances that negatively affect the health of the patient. Furthermore, the government is actively reducing the reproductive health of their inhabitants by using these hemicals, as well as pushing the gay and transgender movement on everyone. I have no problem with these individuals whatsoever, however, this movement is being forced on the children, and so is everything else. In addition, the trans community is under extreme scrutiny by a lot of people, and I applaud them for standing in their power with these people.

The problem with the trans community isn't that it is happening, but now, kids want to change and/or think they re gay at a very young age. Though there is a possibility they ould be, it is however unlikely. The problem really stems from what we are feeding the children, what is being dumped into he air, the media they consume, and what we the adults tell hem. Sexual experiences are also being forced greatly on kids hese days, not to only confuse them about what love truly is, but because historically, it is a way of controlling people. Just hink about it, if a child has a teen pregnancy you will more than likely not go to college and most likely not have much of an ncome, and them being a child still themselves helps to assure hat the cycle continues. I must add that the reasoning behind he trans community and the gay community are much deeper ubjects than what meets the eye. In order to keep a certain level of credibility with certain religious communities, I will not talk about the truth behind majority of the LGBTQ+ community, however, there will come a time I will explain it in much more detail.

There is more poison in the food we eat than ever, and there s an enormous amount of radiation coming through our devices, ell towers and the way our electricity is wired. Our children's education is worse than ever, plus history classes mainly focus on wars. Children today are also massively on the spectrum;

there is a direct correlation between the enormous amounts of vaccines recommended to children to the rate of autism, but this has been pushed under the rug and the statistics reversed. Kids are also very sensitive to these issues; they are like sponges and the information is water. The same goes for racism; no one is born racist, but it is how they are brought up that makes them racist. Another very pressing issue I believe is people are stealing children everywhere; I am certain it is a much deeper subject than what is implied on the news; the narrative is that most of these children are being sold into sex slavery, which I know for sure is not the case, as is also the case with the disappearances of people in wooded areas, as well as the disappearances of Native American women, but that is as far as I will comment. Also, don't let me forget the global warming "crisis".

I would say global warming has been the biggest covert agenda there ever was. Yes, our environment is changing, but it's not because we as individuals are doing things that greatly harm the planet. In fact, the emissions of the world's richest individuals are millions of times higher than what we produce. I understand the need to make electric cars, but the technology we are currently shown is not what is needed to produce these cars. In fact, if you investigate it, it is almost worse for the environment to mine all the materials needed, as well as the production of the batteries, than it is to just use a gas-powered vehicle. The batteries also produce horrible unquenchable fires as well as pollute the landfill when they fail. The real story is that the government wants to control how and when we travel as well as who can afford to; they have the ability to shut down travel whenever they feel like it, with stories of such already out there.

THE TRANSMIGRATE MANIFESTO

Another reason they want to enact these environmental mandates on emissions is they want to make fifteen-minute cities, where everything is available to you within a fifteen-minute walk, bike ride, or public transportation, which is the official Google answer for what a fifteen-minute city is. The inherent problem with creating these cities is that it makes cars seem unnecessary as everything is fifteen minutes away, meaning by spending less money on gas or car maintenance you can save a lot of money, or you can spend more. This will drastically reduce the need for cars causing people to be less mobile, thus controlling the population further. The cities are particularly designed to make the wealthy people the only ones that can travel and afford the price tags. Pay close attention to what the redevelopments in Hawaii are like; there are hidden agendas to all that occurs in society, and very few people pay attention to the ongoing stories that don't directly affect them in the moment, but if it continues to be ongoing, it will directly affect them.

Although they say carbon emissions are the direct causes of global warming, very few scientists realize that the planet is actually a conscious and living being. She has been very patient with us, but it is time to move on from the "third dimension", and she will only take those conscious enough with her to the next dimension. The earth is fighting back against the harm which is being done to her, mainly by our governments who do not care about her or how they are affecting the other living beings on the planet. We have been given enough time now to make these changes, and now is the time the planet will change. Many people have been dying these past few years and the numbers will only increase as the earth begins her commute. The lesson we were supposed to and are learning at the current time is how to love everyone and everything unconditionally, as our planet has been a lovely host; she has reached a point in her existence where it is no longer right to stay in this state of being and allow her life to be destroyed. If you wish to research this further, a good place to start is Dolores Cannon's work who was a past life regression therapist. I will share some of my own past life experiences either in the full version, or the books to come — I will not share what they are about quite yet. One of the agendas of the current controllers of this earth is to act as though they care about our planet, and over the past few years I have realized how much of an agenda it truly is. The government functions as a whole that doesn't care about sustainability or being green; they care about control, and what are the easiest ways to control the population you may wonder? I find this easy to explain through this list:

> 1. Have an overarching control on death, dying, and the afterlife. This is the case for religion, which has been losing its grip slowly over time. Previously, it meant that if you did something "bad" you would be damned to hell, and if you also did not follow the church, you would be ousted from their society, which lessens the chance of survival. Even today, this movement is still infiltrated by government branches in the form of the new age movement, which has a lot of good in it, but at the end of the day, it is still their agenda.

2. Have an overarching control on what people think about. Technology has become very good at controlling our thoughts; just remember all the times you were thinking about buying a product and then you see it on an ad, or maybe someone was talking to you about a product and then it shows up on an ad. Now, this is a simple example you can try, to show how technology controls our thoughts. Think of a banana over the course of a week and notice how many times you see bananas appear on your screens, as well as the word or see them in person. Your brain will also seek out patterns, so the ads you see may also appear because you have become aware of the product; this exercise should show this.

3. Have the people believe "freedom" entails living in the confines of what they say is right and wrong. Have them believe in today's standards of working from nine to five to pay bills, and working overtime to either make ends meet or to have a little bit extra cash to go on a vacation once a year. We did have a lot more freedom than some other countries a couple hundred years ago, but it doesn't work in today's world.

4. Have an overarching control on the media. It is important to control what and how the population sees events including wars. For example, no one talks about the people that fled Ukraine to go to Russia.

5. Have the people believe they are the only people existing in the universe. This is actually a fairly recent

way of viewing the world, as most cultures have some form of extraterrestrial contact in their stories. It wasn't really until the church came into their full power that this way of thinking happened. The same also goes for reincarnation; priests couldn't withstand the hardships they were going through so they killed themselves, and an easy fix for that is to simply remove it. A very important thing to note is the governments are now slowly revealing that we are not alone, although all the three videos released officially were manmade crafts. We have had these crafts since World War Two. I cannot stress this enough, but I believe they are planning a false alien invasion, which there would never be an actual alien invasion, as the earth is very protected by the galactic federation. Although there are problems within the federation, this is not the time to talk about that.

6. Create scenarios just to say that you are the only solution. Just look at recent history, where everyone was pushing for a vaccine to be developed and when it came out, and they were fighting to get it, and tons of them went bad. However, the spread of the virus seemed to go down around that time, even though vaccinated people were still getting sick. Another scenario is the 911 terrorist attack. Without giving too much detail, I believe there is enough evidence to say it was an inside job. Also, the fact that we were not really wanted overseas says a lot, but that is enough talk on that topic for the time being.

7. Control the use of all consumer products. This has both good and bad effects; the good part of this is that harmful material is kept away, while the bad part is that the government controls what we can and can't use, including technology. Know that technology is way more advanced than we can imagine. I've heard someone deep in the military industrial complex say, "Anything you can imagine has been made already." Though I am paraphrasing, it says a lot.

8. The most recurring theme in all of these is fear; keep the people in fear, and they will blindly follow what they are told and will not question it like the good little soldiers we are. A great example is how people blindly followed the COVID mandates. Now for a lot of people with medical issues, it was necessary that they followed some of the mandates. What stuck out to me the most was how uncreative the "controllers" (whoever they truly are) were; the two past big viruses, Ebola and COVID, were both said to originate from bats. The "controllers" tend to use the old way of doing things, no matter how many times it has been done before. Also keep track of where and how the number 72 appears in the media.

I feel I have given enough examples and that the idea of being controlled has been imprinted in your mind. We are dealing with an entity that believes we are blind to these occurrences, and they act in a manner believing we will do nothing against what they are putting the population through. I for one will not allow the occurrences to happen any longer.

To my knowledge, the US 2020 election was rigged large by a collection of spy satellites run by the Vatican, given to the by the Italian government. The interference was large undetectable, thereby causing a lot of backlash towards th Trump administration. Also, to my knowledge, Trump w largely uncorrupted at the start of his presidency, but others the government did not like this, which is why there is so muc hate towards him to this day. The January 6th insurrection w worsened by people hired to stoke the fire, and the same go for the Black Lives Matter riots. Many people don't think twi about the information from the news because of the fear of bein unaccepted. Well, I am glad to say that has changed greatly du to the COVID vaccine backlash. I can boldly say that the 201 US election was clearly rigged in favor of Trump, and if it w not rigged, then people must have really hated Clinton, whic would not be a surprise to me considering the Bernie Sande situation.

Members of the military also clearly did not want Bide in office. At the biggest protest on inauguration day, almost a the soldiers had their backs turned to the presidential escor Also, Biden was not informed of all ongoing military operation which makes me believe there is so much more to the stor than what is being told, but the media does not want to cove it. I believe Trump knows a lot more of what is going on tha what is shown on television and that is why he was trying to d something against the agendas. So, in order to stop Trump, the created so much backlash against him in the government an media. I do not believe Trump has completely pure intentions but he has better intentions than any recent president has had; the man was a billionaire in office, so naturally, his intention would be about making more money which is both beneficial and detrimental to the American people.

Currently, the biggest problem with America is the voter. Even though the elections are rigged, the people's votes do affect the outcome in some way. There was no way the Bush family would have been voted into office if people did any form of background on them. George H.W. Bush Sr. was the head of the CIA and the vice president of Ronald Reagan, but very few people know of the true story behind his family's origin and the story of his vice presidency. His initials H.W., as well as his name were from his maternal grandfather and banker, George Herbert Walker, who directly helped to fund the Nazis, which at the time wasn't seen as treason. At that time, the United States wanted to join the Nazis, and for simple evidence, Hitler was the man of the year for Time magazine in 1938. The plot to join the Germans was put to a stop when Franklin Roosevelt was one of the few to realize what was going on — his plan Pearl Harbor. Roosevelt sent a hundred and two ships into the harbor to try and pressure Japan to attack; they did attack and only two ships were destroyed, and all the other ships were repaired. Something kept fairly hidden from the American people was the fact that Japan was in peace talks with the United States before the use of atomic weaponry. The reason we dropped two bombs was pure spite over the Japanese ruining our plans for joining the Axis. This was one of the biggest what ifs in history and if we did not have the leaders we did at the time, history would have been very different. Bush, being the head of the CIA had a lot of knowledge of what was going on, including illegal operations, and to ensure that it remains hidden, he decided to become president. He did so not just for one term, as he needed to rule for a longer period, so he became vice president to an actor. The real truth behind that term was Reagan acted as a puppet for Bush so he was able to hide a lot of bad ordeals. Of course, he later became president for real for one term, and his kid for two terms. The CIA has made dealings in a lot of really bad actions in the name of "democracy" and money. I will leave the subject here for you the reader, to do your own research on the matter.

The Hypocrisy of Our Controllers

The hypocrisy in our government is hysterical. They act as though we do not have eyes to see and ears to hear, as our cities burn in the name of equality and our troops die in the name of freedom, terrorism, oil, or... The American people are constantly realizing and understanding more of what is going on, so the government tries to change the narrative by calling everyone else conspiracy theorists. The Americans as a whole are not completely blind to what is going on, but we are easily tricked into believing their narratives which further splits we the people.

It is only our controllers who can tell us what we can and cannot believe; only our controllers can tell us who we will love and who we will hate; only our controllers can antagonize the ransacking of towns but kill innocent people to get what they want; only our controllers can tell us what we can and cannot eat and drink; only our controllers can proclaim they are saints while the world grows restless; only our controllers can decide what technology we can have; only our controllers can ban substances that increase our awareness while promoting consuming ones that prohibit our awareness; only our controllers can shut down the world by paralyzing everyone with crippling fear and anxiety; only our controllers can wage proxy war; only our controllers are allowed to produce drugs to sell;

only our controllers get tax breaks; only our controllers can create natural disasters through weather manipulation, in order to take control of a region; only our controllers can manufacture terrorist attacks to sway the public into going to war; only our controllers can impose one religion is the end all be all; only our controllers can raid museums in Iraq to steal thousands of artifacts; only our controllers can know about the Egyptian artifacts found in the grand canyon; only our controllers can know about the artifacts hidden by the Smithsonian institute; only our controllers can take young men and make them killing machines; only our controllers can attack countries in the name of democracy, only to need these men for other wars; only our controllers can create large documents to hide what is truly inside of them; only our controllers can feed the people poison and war, while they sit idly by with watchful eyes unaffected; only our controllers can purposely delay military aid in the country to try and incite riots and then enact martial law; only our controllers are unable to process the amount of love we can have as a species for each other; only our controllers wish to divide us through religious beliefs, political parties, skin color, gender, and language.

Only our controllers in the past were allowed to make decisions for us based on a couple of choices, most of which we did not actually get to vote on what we actually thought. Only our controllers can impose on us the right way to do things. Well, I'm here to tell you it does not have to be that way. Don't you want to follow your dreams effortlessly, and not be confined to a nine to five life. Don't you want to live in a world where the government doesn't control what you can and cannot do, because it goes against how far evolved they are. Don't you want live in a world where you can work on what you want to work on and do not have to answer to a self-proclaimed higher power? I know I do; this is the basics which I believe can be a groundwork for a new government. However, the only way to make these changes is if you raise your own consciousness and love for yourself and others, and not in an egotistical way. Love your body and mind enough to realize the injustices that are being brought upon you. Although it may seem like you are the victim, I promise you are not, and all it takes to break free from these injustices is to realize you were the one putting yourself in these situations. Now, you may say to yourself, "I didn't choose where I was born or to who I was born to", and to that, I say think again. I am of the firm belief that we are all exactly where we need to be at any given moment; one, to help others out and two, to help ourselves. If you were to realize you are the victim of your own thoughts, you would realize that you don't need the government's rules and regulations, because you would quickly realize the system doesn't work for you. If you just stopped to realize you do not want to work for all these hours, or want to pay for fuel or water to drink, or pay taxes on the energy you spent slaving away, or pay taxes on the products you buy with your taxed energy, you would realize this system neither works in your favor, nor has it for a long time.

If you were to pay attention to your body when you eat or drink anything, you would quickly realize what does and does not nourish you. For me, this was the first realization that I am something more than a worker bee. I realized I had problems with certain foods, which were horribly affecting my health, so by looking deeper into that, I started to get the bigger picture of what the government was truly doing to us. After a few years

of paying attention to my thoughts and my body, those foo
do not affect me that much anymore, because what science h
failed to realize is just how much consciousness affects yo
health and everything around you. Once you realize you are
control of your thoughts, you will be truly free to think ar
speak. If you think you are the victim, then you are, but only
yourself. You have the ability to be angry or sad, and therefor
you have the ability to decide what makes you angry or sad. Mo
of the time, being angry or sad is a result of being lost in tl
story. Of course, sadness and anger do have their place, either i
grieving or being fueled to make change, but if you are sad c
angry about a situation for more than forty-five seconds, the
you are lost in the story you are telling yourself.

It is only a natural evolution of learning material c
conscious nature, that you will want to help others out, becau:
you will begin to realize just how close we all actually are, an
why we need a government that reflects these thoughts an
feelings.

Changes to the Government

I do not wish to start fresh as there are a lot of good traits and great people working in it, so my new government would follow a lot of what is already being done, though it is ratified and purposefully designed to be abolished at some point in the future — not necessarily in its entirety. There would still be local governments and public works, as well as some kind of police and fire force designed especially for special cases, which I have outlined further ahead. But I also see the actual government not having much to do apart from dealing with forces of nature and the military. Afterwards, I would assume a lot of the scientific advancements would be done by people who genuinely care about what they are researching. I mean, all research wouldn't be forced upon people just because we have to research something for funding, but rather because it will be used for the good of humanity. Money will largely be a thing of the past; people will resort to bartering and good will for services, while money would be used as a last resort. People will also only work as many hours per week as they desire to. Probably, at the beginning not much will change, which is good because, it has to be a slow transition, where the right people would have to be the ones in charge, and be individuals the people can actually trust to take care of not only our current country, but be able to set an example that will lead the world into a united place.

This transition will have to start somewhere so I suggest we'd take a couple weeks to gather all the information to discover what is actually going on in the world, the truth about extraterrestrials, the technology the military industrial complex has and the civilian purposes of it, and whatever else kind of discoveries that need to be revealed. The country would continue normally at this point, as the new government is being formed. If I was forming the government, I would have the best social thinkers get together to make sure every race, every religion and every gender is included. I may not agree with the entirety of the LGBTQ+ community but that is part of our country and everyone deserves a say, however will that say be approved by the people? That is yet to be seen.

Following the revealing phase, the people of the new country would be presented the ideas made for the country on the first day of the week, through their phones or city halls gatherings that would be voted on at the end of the week. There would also be papers sent out to everyone at home so they can read the presentation, and not have to worry about going out twice a week. There would also be some kind of mail in ballet which would have to be dropped off or sent to the city hall and received by the end of Saturday night; Sunday would be the counting day and Monday, the new presentation will be delivered as well as announcements of what happened, which again papers would be sent out. Everyone from the age of sixteen and upwards will be allowed to vote on the matters. Following the voting sessions, the work that was promised to be done will begin and the things that didn't get two-thirds vote will be ratified or thrown out depending on the voting results.

THE TRANSMIGRATE MANIFESTO

As the voting is taking place and the people deciding the ideas for the new government are thinking, there would be councils of people who would be working on making that idea a reality. That idea for example, could be automatic farming if it has been discovered by the military industrial complex, as well as producing self-navigating semis, with the aim of making food free, which isn't the furthest stretch of the imagination. Assuming these technologies exist, just like the self-driving vehicles are. The military industrial complex knows how to use infinite energy, so that could be worked on alongside using that technology for vehicle production, home, and factory uses, thereby making travel, and power free, and reduce food costs. All these things would certainly take time to do, and for a little while, life would continue to be fairly close to how it is now. That is unless a large amount of people want to help these efforts, which may be the case, but over time, we would reduce wages due to the free cost of living and have as many people who desire to build homes for the homeless, and create jobs for the jobless. Subsequently, money would not really equate to much; it may slowly on its own have less of an influence as people will naturally want to do things differently and help others along on their journey. Also, with all this newfound time, they would pick up hobbies and naturally start bartering, with money becoming a secondary thought to the people, used only when there is no other source of payment. There would be minimal taxes as most of the work would be volunteer work and not mandatory; the taxes would be used for funding foreign trade and creation of the new infrastructure, as long as they are approved by the people. With people desiring to help freely, jobs would be filled if they need be, even if they only help for a few hours a week. I envision a system at the end of the day where people will voluntarily take out taxes maybe 10-20% or have it completely by choice how much an individual wants to give, but again this is at the end of the road. The reduction of taxes could surely be done immediately, however leaving it up to vote we may decide to keep the status quo in order to pay the people reconstructing society. Also since taxes are governmental it should be made entirely public whether an individual pays taxes or not.

Once all the details are sorted out, people can now discover who they are and hopefully, the rest of the world would see what is going on, leading to the committee that made the new government helping out other nations, and maybe uniting nations. Once everyone gets a feel for things in life — maybe five or ten years after completion — the government would be worked on again to provide more freedom for the people who feel constrained. This would eventually lead to the true new government where everyone basically feels free; the problem is the rest of the world, are they at this point? The country might have to be stuck in limbo for a while, while other nations catch up, and they would eventually. It is only then can the world be unified and after this unity can the government can be put to full use, and eventually dissolved and reworked, if need be.

I see the world working in a series of councils. Every city has a council where they talk about problems and its solutions; anyone can be in these councils, and everyone can pitch ideas to the council. If it is a country-wide problem, the city council would then vote on a certain number of ideas and suggest them to the county, who would then vote on its city's ideas. From there, a certain number of those ideas would be taken to the state level, and depending on how it gets worked out, either a few of ıe county members would show up to the state capital to vote, r there would be council members elected into the state level ɔ vote on what they think are the best ideas. They would then ιke these ideas to the capital where the high council will vote n the best ones from around the country or world, depending n how the government develops. The president or whatever he/ ıe may be called if there is one at all, would oversee the voting, nd from what the capital decides are the best solutions, the resident would then pick what he thinks is the best idea, or he ıay be there just to be the tie breaker. That may be where the rocess ends, unless we want further steps, where the people vote n either what the high council decides, or what the president ecides, and if there is no president and there is a tie the people ıay vote on the selected choices. It may also be that the resident wouldn't decide at all, but the people and councils onsider their input on the matter. The issues of the country or vorld may also just plainly be voted upon by the high council n the behalf of the people. The problem that may arise in the eginning stages if this were to occur would be corruption, vhich is why I'd say for the start let the ideas of all flow. verything the high council voted upon would have its members xplain why they voted in that way so that all may see the easoning, this too will make sure there is no corruption. If we re the only country at the time changing, having invested nterest in a foreign country will affect decision making, and as t should but there should be no lies that this is being done. For ninor instances, the city councils would vote and that would be t; they would either select a few ideas for the people to vote on ɔr one for an answer Again, the council would be made up of ɔeople in the city or the elected state council or the president

could even sit in on the voting as well. If decisions directly affe
other cities or counties, they would also get a say in the matter.

Now, the question is what stays and what goes? To sta
off, I don't know if I would change too much at one time. Th
country may appear weak to other nations, depending on th
real conflicts they encounter, because I'm sure most of the wa
they have fought in the past have been more than just a surfa
level hate. Nations wage war to benefit either monetarily or
benefit their agendas, but my assumption is we would be playir
a defensive game unless the other nations were changing at th
same time, which is unlikely but not impossible. To r
knowledge, all three letter agencies spend only 10-15% of the
time and resources actually helping the people of the countr
and the rest is spent doing things that directly or indirectly har
us.

The core activities of the FBI would stay for the time bein
as laws are reworked. I would shatter the CIA into a thousan
pieces — a paraphrase from JFK. I would also strip down th
NRO, and the rest of these agencies, I would look into reducin
them. I feel there is a lot of corruption in all of the three lette
agencies, so I would want to make arrangements to have ther
investigated. We wouldn't need congress; I would keep th
Judicial branch and get rid of Executive and Legislative branche
The problem arises if we are the only country who is changin
because there may be attacks on our soil due to the destructio
of these agencies, the problem is they are so corrupt they nee
to be, the big issue with these organizations is lack of citize
oversight we may create new agencies if we so desire bu
everything needs to be public. There may be a president wh
would oversee the project, but if no one is just and fair and ca

fill the spot and make the tough choices that will follow the freedom that ensues after the creation of the new government, I would get rid of that position. There should be someone who the people can trust who would be their leader until they retire, die, or get voted out; the term limit would most likely not be needed in our society. The Judicial branch would be used to make new laws; these laws would not be restrictive, except along the lines of murder, abuse of all kinds, and for cracking down on drugs. The simple answer to the drug problem is not allowing the creation of them to begin with, we shall not penalize someone for taking an addictive drug, we must nurture these individuals back to health not lock them away. I don't mean psychoactive drugs as they are really pointless to ban—they were prior because the government doesn't want people to use them and have spiritual awakenings, causing them to realize what the government is actually doing to its people, this is exactly what should be encouraged in our society. The punishments — like therapy — wouldn't be bad, and I'm sure there would arise better ways of handling mental illnesses but the problem with drug makers usually is the money it brings in. If we design our society as previously mentioned where money isn't that important because it is not needed to live, a lot of these issues will be resolved by themselves, making it hard to predict what is and is not an issue. Now, if an offense is repeated and therapy isn't helping, then in my mind sending the person to jail/prison is understandable but only as a way of watching an individual. Prisons today are a way of "punishing" an individual for doing a crime, but all it does is remove them from society and place them into an institution where everyone has gone mad. But there may be better options out there that someone would think of, and that is the reasoning behind the new government, cooperation of the people in the creation o new ideas. Also, in my mind, I see that this form o "punishment" would continue to be used in the future, there will always be mental issues that need to be resolved, as of righ now it is just a fact of life, it can change and it will if we follow this path, but for the foreseeable future this is an adequate "punishment". I would also keep the DNR and the National Parks program and see what we could do to help these programs further. The hope is that we would grow to become one with nature and not live in giant concrete cities. Also, there would be almost no pollution in the cities, but it is still not good to do. If the population stays the same or grows — which I actually think it will decline — then maybe we can make nature more of a part of these cities and we can at least attempt something. I would also allow guns, semi-automatic, and as time progresses and morality changes in the world, I would drop the ban on automatic weapons. Now, worst case scenario, if we are raided by other nations, that would be a different story. I also think that mental health would become extremely better for a multitude of reasons, so I really only see benefits of owning firearms in the case that we are the only country allowing more freedom. If there are better alternatives, those would be allowed too, if not immediately, then down the road. I would assume there are indeed better alternatives like involving electromagnetism, plasma, lasers, and/or frequency weaponry, but that is not entirely important at the moment.

As morality improves in the people of the new founded government, further power shall be given to them, with only the necessary agencies remaining, including but not limited to, national and local park preservation and building — a form of

DNR. However, as the morality of the people improves, these agencies may not be required such as law enforcement agencies aiming to help those in need, public works and local government, which would be used for the betterment of the people, and not used to create or force restrictions, except in publicly voted upon special cases; and military powers used for the defense of the people from other nations. A series of checks and balances must be worked out for the military, as well as making all that is being worked on in the military industrial complex known to the population, and adapted for civilian use. A special council of ecopolitical affairs would have to be workshopped and voted upon, including other people of the world even if they are not apart of the council or similar free system. If we decide to not have dealings with other races, we shall revote on the decision every so often. My opinion on the matter is that we ask for guidance concerning the formation of our new government and how to deal with the other governments of the world. They may also not help until the whole world is united. Whatever the case, my vote would be to develop our country on our own, with the exception of help in the form of guidance.

The school system would teach kids true history as well as new history. As the world progresses forward from today, you will see that history is not actually what you were told, and the true history of our people would be learned and taught. Mathematics would be changed to reflect what we know from the military industrial complex, as well as what we learn from the advancement of society. There should be books made and read that make the students question morality, not only for themselves but so they may never end up in the mess we are in today ever again. As secrets are unearthed, what we teach in schools would have to be seriously changed to reflect what we know. Also, a council of scholars would need to be created to determine what should be taught in schools, in addition to the most effective ways of doing so. When the decision to integrate more galactically comes about, this may be changed again. It would all depend on the decisions of other councils and how much we would integrate. I can confidently say that there are beings currently working against earth and her evolution, but we are immensely protected, and I do not see any issues with extraterrestrials, except in the event of a false flag invasion.

As people of the world become wiser, the need for schooling would be reduced. I see a world where most of the learning would be done on the job, even in the world of surgery. I still see the need to study parts of the body and how it reacts to different substances, however I do not believe that as we progress in life more as a society, there would not be the need to attend college for jobs. I'm not saying that you shouldn't go to college for work, but I think college can take up more of a higher learning role than what it is now. Higher learning means furthering one's wisdom and intellect in an environment where people with higher knowledge on a particular subject can come and deliver lectures; these people would be paid either in the form of service or monetarily, depending on how we advance as a country and what they need.

I also see our new world government needing leaders, and I believe every person alive at some point in our future can be a leader, or can at least have some ideas for society and how to benefit it. This is why I see the council system that I mentioned before, working the best for society. I believe that system, as well all the other things I have talked about, should be up for a very healthy debate. I encourage anyone with other ideas to either speak out about them now or speak out about them if/when the time comes for our new government. It can only help to share ideas and debate these topics. I understand there will be a lot of negativity to these ideas as well, mainly from negative people, but if you have ideas, great, if not, your hate will forever and always be pointless.

The Declaration of Independence
Today

To further my cause, I included the Declaration of Independence. I bolded the grievances that are being directly done against us. I have also underlined the ones that don't apply to us, either because of the laws that were put in place during the creation of the country, or they are just outdated. I will not elaborate in this version, except where it's absolutely necessary, however in the full version, I plan to do something special with the Declaration of Independence. Since we are not parliament, the meaning does need to change, so keep that in mind. Again, this is just to show what is being done against us, this is not a Declaration of Independence.

In Congress, July 4, 1776

The unanimous Declaration

The unanimous Declaration of the thirteen united States of America, When in the Course of human events, it becomes necessary for one people to dissolve the political bands which have connected them with another, and to assume among the powers of the earth, the separate and equal station to which the Laws of Nature and of Nature's God entitle them, a decent respect to the opinions of mankind requires that they should declare the causes which impel them to the separation.

THE TRANSMIGRATE MANIFESTO

We hold these truths to be self-evident, that all men are created equal, that they are endowed by their Creator with certain unalienable Rights, that among these are Life, Liberty and the pursuit of Happiness.—That to secure these rights, Governments are instituted among Men, deriving their just powers from the consent of the governed,—That whenever any Form of Government becomes destructive of these ends, it is the Right of the People to alter or to abolish it, and to institute new Government, laying its foundation on such principles and organizing its powers in such form, as to them shall seem most likely to effect their Safety and Happiness. Prudence, indeed, will dictate that Governments long established should not be changed for light and transient causes; and accordingly, all experience hath shewn, that mankind are more disposed to suffer, while evils are sufferable, than to right themselves by abolishing the forms to which they are accustomed. But when a long train of abuses and usurpations, pursuing invariably the same Object evinces a design to reduce them under absolute Despotism, it is their right, it is their duty, to throw off such Government, and to provide new Guards for their future security.—Such has been the patient sufferance of these Colonies; and such is now the necessity which constrains them to alter their former Systems of Government. The history of the present King of Great Britain is a history of repeated injuries and usurpations, all having in direct object the establishment of an absolute Tyranny over these States. To prove this, let Facts be submitted to a candid world.

He has refused his Assent to Laws, the most wholesome and necessary for the public good.

He has forbidden his Governors to pass Laws of immediate and pressing importance, unless suspended in their operation till his Assent should be obtained; and when so suspended, he has utterly neglected to attend to them. (This mainly entails the two-party system not allowing laws to be passed that need to be).

He has refused to pass other Laws for the accommodation of large districts of people, unless those people would relinquish the right of Representation in the Legislature, a right inestimable to them and formidable to tyrants only. (This is half true, we vote people into office however most of their true agendas are masked in secrecy).

He has called together legislative bodies at places unusual, uncomfortable, and distant from the depository of their public Records, for the sole purpose of fatiguing them into compliance with his measures. (The compliance with measures is true but in a different way, such as when the country gave Trump crap for not signing the covid relief, which was a huge packet of paper, where we were giving more aid per person to other countries than our own. We only received $600 while other countries were getting thousands per person, based on the money we gave them).

He has dissolved Representative Houses repeatedly, for opposing with manly firmness his invasions on the rights of the people. (This is partially correct, this is about unfair taxation without the people's consent, which yes, we vote in our officials, but we do not really get much of a say).

He has refused for a long time, after such dissolutions, to cause others to be elected; whereby the Legislative powers, incapable of Annihilation, have returned to the People at large for their exercise; the State remaining in the meantime exposed to all the dangers of invasion from without, and convulsions within.

He has endeavored to prevent the population of these States; for that purpose obstructing the Laws for Naturalization of Foreigners; refusing to pass others to encourage their migrations hither, and raising the conditions of new Appropriations of Lands.

He has obstructed the Administration of Justice, by refusing his Assent to Laws for establishing Judiciary powers.

He has made Judges dependent on his Will alone, for the tenure of their offices, and the amount and payment of their salaries. (There are and have been judges that have been paid off to vote one way or the other, however this statement is outdated).

He has erected a multitude of New Offices, and sent hither swarms of Officers to harass our people, and eat out their substance.

He has kept among us, in times of peace, Standing Armies without the Consent of our legislatures. (Although technically correct we are an army of our own people).

He has affected to render the Military independent of and superior to the Civil power. (Military Industrial Complex as well as Marshal Law, which I didn't get into but there were times they have tried to incite it purposefully).

He has combined with others to subject us to a jurisdiction foreign to our constitution, and unacknowledged by our laws; giving his Assent to their Acts of pretended Legislation:

For Quartering large bodies of armed troops among us:

For protecting them, by a mock Trial, from punishment for any Murders which they should commit on the Inhabitants of these States:

For cutting off our Trade with all parts of the world:

For imposing Taxes on us without our Consent:

<u>**For depriving us in many cases, of the benefits of Trial by Jury:**</u> (This is more so trial by fair jury which occurred and sometimes still occurs).

<u>For transporting us beyond Seas to be tried for pretended offenses</u>

<u>For abolishing the free System of English Laws in a neighboring Province, establishing therein an Arbitrary government, and enlarging its Boundaries so as to render it at once an example and fit instrument for introducing the same absolute rule into these Colonies:</u> (We could be seen as the ones doing this now and in the past to other nations).

<u>**For taking away our Charters, abolishing our most valuable Laws, and altering fundamentally the Forms of our Governments:**</u>

<u>**For suspending our own Legislatures, and declaring themselves invested with power to legislate for us in all cases whatsoever.**</u> (This is really to the people who have acted against the government in peaceful ways that were seen as a threat, so they were removed).

<u>He has abdicated Government here, by declaring us out of his Protection and waging War against us.</u>

He has plundered our seas, ravaged our Coasts, burnt our towns, and destroyed the lives of our people.

He is at this time transporting large Armies of foreign Mercenaries to complete the works of death, desolation and

tyranny, already begun with circumstances of Cruelty & perfidy scarcely paralleled in the most barbarous ages, and totally unworthy the Head of a civilized nation. (Waging proxy wars).

He has constrained our fellow Citizens taken Captive on the high Seas to bear Arms against their Country, to become the executioners of their friends and Brethren, or to fall themselves by their Hands.

He has excited domestic insurrections amongst us, and has endeavored to bring on the inhabitants of our frontiers, the merciless Indian Savages, whose known rule of warfare, is an undistinguished destruction of all ages, sexes and conditions. (The exciting of riots).

In every stage of these Oppressions, we have Petitioned for Redress in the most humble terms: Our repeated Petitions have been answered only by repeated injury. A Prince whose character is thus marked by every act which may define a Tyrant, is unfit to be the ruler of a free people.

Nor have We been wanting in attentions to our British brethren. We have warned them from time to time of attempts by their legislature to extend an unwarrantable jurisdiction over us. We have reminded them of the circumstances of our emigration and settlement here. We have appealed to their native justice and magnanimity, and we have conjured them by the ties of our common kindred to disavow these usurpations, which, would inevitably interrupt our connections and correspondence. They too have been deaf to the voice of justice and of consanguinity. We must, therefore, acquiesce in the necessity, which denounces our Separation, and hold them, as we hold the rest of mankind, Enemies in War, in Peace Friends.

We, therefore, the Representatives of the united States of America, in General Congress, Assembled, appealing to the Supreme Judge of the world for the rectitude of our intentions do, in the Name, and by Authority of the good People of these Colonies, solemnly publish and declare, That these United Colonies are, and of Right ought to be Free and Independent States; that they are Absolved from all Allegiance to the British Crown, and that all political connection between them and the State of Great Britain, is and ought to be totally dissolved; and that as Free and Independent States, they have full Power to levy War, conclude Peace, contract Alliances, establish Commerce, and to do all other Acts and Things which Independent States may of right do. And for the support of this Declaration, with a firm reliance on the protection of divine Providence, we mutually pledge to each other our Lives, our Fortunes and our sacred Honor.

My Message to the Future People of Earth

Although the world of today is not what it should be, you can be the change you wish to see in the world. I understand that changing a system that so many people hold dear seems like an impossible task, however at some point as a society, we must notice we are in a toxic relationship with our controllers. This does not need to be an aggressive revolution; all it takes is for enough people to say enough is enough and take a stand. I don't expect to see these changes happening overnight and a lot of the systems we have in place will take time to reform. Of course, a large part of that reformation is giving time for people to research what is going on behind the scenes. You can't come up with solutions if you are using the same state of consciousness that created them in the first place. All it takes is for anyone with eyes to see, to do the research and take a stand based on their findings. However, information is more lucrative than you may think, and a lot of the information available has been suppressed, hidden by algorithms, or changed to fit with what the controllers are imposing. It is therefore going to take all of us banding together and taking a stand in the name of love for our fellow man, as well as the love for our planet and most importantly, our fate as a civilization. It is not my job to start these events, but it is my job to guide people into seeing the light at the end of the tunnel. It is therefore up to other individuals to take that stand for what is right for all in all areas of life. If you the reader decides to do nothing with what you have learned either through this working, the next working, or the research you have done because of the working, then I have done all I can do. This means, I have tried to lead the horse on a long journey to water, but that horse has neither the thirst nor the will to progress onward. However, if the reader of this work decides to take a stand, then my work would have begun to advise the future humans in their pursuit of knowledge, love, and oneness, and there is no greater honor in the universe.

If we continue to do nothing with the knowledge we have we will continue to be suppressed, and killed off either through the chemicals, food, and radiation we ingest and put on and in our bodies, or through our own wanting to not pursue romantic relationships. Stop eating food that has been in plastic containers, and don't be afraid to say no to others when they offer something potentially harmful. If we continue to let the controllers take liberties that are not theirs to possess, we as a species will quickly die off, and not only through previous mentions, but the earth also herself is a conscious being who will no longer stand the injustices done to her and her people. I see the year of 2024 and onward having many natural disasters until change is made, and if we allow this path to continue, things will get worse, and the earth will start to push back harder and harder. There will be a lot of changes here on earth and she has no quarrel with moving on without us; although she is doing all she can do to move on with us, it is up to us to make that decision.

It will take everything in everyone to change, I hope we can all realize our problems, personally and globally. If you are blocking the world out with drugs and alcohol, now is the time to come clean. To the ones who do not realize they are doing this, take note of when you are consuming these items, including sugar, which has been a big problem in my life. I personally struggled with sugar consumption and depression in high school, it would numb my emotions, and love for others brought me out of it. Throughout high school I was wildly unchallenged even in all the AP classes. I would never take homework home because I would get it done effortlessly in class, nor would I study for tests ever. Around my junior year I noticed my health started to decline, and I slowly became more depressed, causing life to become harder for me. It didn't help that I felt out of place, I would wear hoodies to tune people out, developing the nickname school shooter from some. I didn't have much to pull me through except for my friends and video games, however junior year the friend group split, leaving me, my cousin, and another friend for playing games together, occasionally the others would play, but it was a hard time for me. To add to it all, I did not enjoy the restaurant I worked at, I only stayed for the other people there. Eventually someone came to work there that I started to really like, and we started dating a little into junior year. School was hard for me to want to be there, and I didn't enjoy the company of really anyone from school except for five people; three of which I didn't talk to out of school, one was my best friend since kindergarten, and one I never spoke to at all, our connection being shared past lives. I made it through my junior and senior year, the reduction of the more toxic food in my diet slowly changed my outlook on life. The biggest help for me was the love for my friends and partner, as well as the laughs we shared. Through my experience I have realized just how much substances can affect who we are as people, as well as how love can pull us through. If you or someone is struggling with abuse or depression, reach out to them, it is the love we share for one another that will get us through these times.

If we do something to stop our behind-the-scenes controllers, we can finally live freely in a world designed with love for one another in mind. We can slowly make a world with no need for money aside trading for things that your specialties can't buy. We can finally live in a world free to explore and expand in terms of science, math, history, exploration, and consciousness. We are the children of the future. We have been given by our ancestors a conundrum they could not solve; they pushed their problems onto the children of tomorrow, and now that tomorrow has come, what will you do, and how will you do it? Will you fall back into the negative thoughts our controllers impose? Will you decide that enough is enough? Will you allow love into your cold heart? Will you become the change you wish to see in the world? Will you be the one standing on the front lines of true democracy? Will you be an example for the rest of the world and the universe to model? Will you become who you were meant to be at this time, politically or not? Your next question should be how much of my time shall I dedicate to this work if I have something to share? The answer is very simple, all of it. We are running out of time to stop what is coming, so you the reader needs to be the one who changes yourself and in doing so, it will bring changes to the world around you that you cannot even imagine. This revolution needs to happen peacefully, as why would you want to build a country founded on love for one another on blood?

THE TRANSMIGRATE MANIFESTO

I encourage as many people as possible to read this. Please, if you can share this work, talk about it, and debate it. Maybe this work would spark something either in you or someone you share with. My only wishes are that we the people would become wiser to what is being done to us and do something about it. I hope this opportunity to act is not lost by those who feel inspired to act and do not.

Sincerely,

Keegan Beaton

freedomowl.com

Helpful Resources

1. *Cia.gov* - there are tons of declassified documents that ca
be retrieved on this site.

2. *Gaia tv* - there is a lot of material here; it is a pai
subscription, and it is very useful. Daniel Sheehan has some gre
interviews with Regina Merideth that I highly recommend yo
have give a listen to.

3. Channeled material of all kinds; take whoever resonate
with you, as well as whatever information resonates with you.

4. Look into the assassination of JFK; it will open your eye
to a lot of what has been happening in the background.

5. Study metaphysics, as this will be useful in understandin
the full manifesto.

6. Study the CIA declassified documents on the gatewa
project, as this will be useful in understanding the full manifest

7. Study Dolores Cannon's books, especially for Christians
listen or read *Jesus and the Essenes* and *They Walked With Jesus*, a
this will be useful in understanding the full manifesto.

8. Dr. Steven Greer is a good person to start studyin
extraterrestrials from, as this will be useful in understanding th
full manifesto.

9. Cosmic Agency on YouTube (start from the beginning)
I do not agree with all the material, but they are mainly lookin
outside in and not inside out, as we are. This source particularl

resonated with me; it is like all information I had learned before became irrelevant. I believe that is because the nature of this information is purer than others, and our bodies can sense that and will tell us. This resource will be useful for understanding the full manifesto.

There are hundreds of other resources, but I cannot remember most of them, nor would it be entirely helpful as everyone learns differently. If you are meant and determined to find out further information about a subject, you will; I urge everyone to dig deeper and start asking questions. I have found that every question I have ever asked, I received an answer. The biggest question one can ask is, who am I? The answer would lead you down a very convoluted rabbit hole of self-realization and self-betterment. With that, I wish you all well, and we shall speak soon in my full-length vision.

Novi Populi Ordinis

THE TRANSMIGRATE MANIFESTO

The society of today is a shell of what it once was. We no longer lend a hand, trade and break bread with, nor pray and commune with our neighbor. Today we perceive ourselves too busy to meet our neighbor, or worse we fear them. Our society has gone from that of community to that of consuming. We used to produce our own food, build our own buildings, sheer our own sheep, and for the commodities that which we didn't produce we would trade or give to each other knowing they would do the same. I do not say this to encourage a certain lifestyle or bash anyone for not living like this, as the society of consumerism that we live in now is a double-edged sword as is community living.

Community living was required for our physical survival in our past which is what causes us to be so anxious and concerned with what people think of us. If we take a look at older people in how they act, we can see how life should be lived. From what I've noted is that older people say what's actually on their mind because they stopped caring what others think about them for the most part. The reasoning is they start thinking they'll die soon anyways so might as well not waste time hiding how they feel, even if the thought of dying is only at a subconscious level it still affects how they perceive reality. If we adopted this mentality ourselves, what risks and actions would we take? How much would our lives change if we would only stop concerning ourselves with what others thought about us? Now it's sad but I must add I'm not saying these words to the ones who wish to perform harmful actions to others, I'm saying them to the ones who wish to perform loving, energetic, and youthful actions to others and themselves. I believe that Covid was a great teacher in this subject. Although it may have seemed like a curse while we were all locked in our homes, really it has been a blessing in disguise. Without the constant influence of society on our psyches, it eroded our egos to try and teach us what is truly important in our lives. Now not everyone has had the same experience, I wasn't short of work so I was still outgoing, but my disillusionment came in different ways. I have never thought like normal individuals, as I would describe the way I think like I am channeling myself. What is channeling? A simple description is your consciousness leaves your physical shell you call your body and another one comes in, this is not the way it is done for everyone who does channeling but it is a basic description. This is how it feels with my mind I'm not fully in the body and I see through facades, it makes making friends and talking a lot of the time very difficult especially after my ego death; post ego death everything I hear and say sounds unintelligent because words themselves are actually a limitation in communication and as we progresses through this work you too shall understand why that is. Since I feel like I'm constantly channeling myself school was really easy for me, which really just burnt me out from wanting to go to college, which in consequence unintentionally sent me down a path I could have never even imagined. Thus is the purpose for disillusionment, to bring you to true creation, I went from a very uncreative thinker to having so many ideas I could never accomplish them all.

In a world designed for mediocrity we are instilled the factory production mindset from age four, and when you don't conform to the standard you are told you have problems only medicine can fix. I acted out personally in elementary school I noticed the concern in others so I controlled my behavior in middle school and on. A part of that is my mind works more in ircles for instance, if I were to say "The dog was red." I may think "Red was the dog." It causes me to slur my speech sometimes, but the benefit to this is I think at different angles with different ideas allowing me to learn fairly easily. I believe that the kids who are told they have issues just aren't set up to think in the conventional way, meaning the way school is currently set up just doesn't work for them.

Being told you have problems can have a massive impact on ones self esteem causing an even larger impact on the difficulty to perform tasks at a satisfactory level. Having low self-esteem also causes anxiety affecting everything you do, making something as simple as ordering food a hassle. Another issue with low self-esteem is the looking up to the models of the world who also have the same issues, paired with doom scrolling actually worsens their mental condition. A little known fact of existence is that we leave our energetic imprint on our creations and it is felt by the observer while viewing said creation. So when a model who is so concerned with their body and has bad experiences with trying to look good posts something online for the world to see, it is felt, causing the viewer to also feel that way within themselves. At a one post level it really doesn't have too much of an affect, the problems arise when you are constantly consuming this type of media. I believe the kids in the classroom today and those of tomorrow will continue to have an increase of self-esteem issues caused by technology, which will also cause the kids who do not appear different to start to see the kids around them changing, more than likely causing them to develop self-esteem issues, perpetuating the problem for everyone. The ones with issues will see the ones without and call them insane when truly it is the other way around. The circular thinking and the inability to quiet down the constant mental chatter the very reasoning behind senility, dementia, and Alzheime however the medical field is designed to disregard thoughts as creative device, or in this case destruction device. This is calle losing your mind, think of a mad scientist who is constant uttering nonsense or talks in circles, this is the reasoning fc these diseases, as is the reasoning behind why people younge and younger are getting these diseases.

We are teaching our kids to conform by making them more soulless version of which we already have perpetuatin the problems already occurring. The material we are teaching i our classrooms only worsens the problems we already have. Th biggest lie taught in the classroom today is climate change due t carbon emissions, plants need carbon to live, the problem with i occurs because we removed so many trees it does have an impac however the big reason is the big companies emissions. A bi issue with the removal of trees is how nonsensical it is we coul very easily use hemp for paper and clothing, but it wouldn't b nearly as profitable which is why its just outright banned, w have been able to farm it recently but only after all of the damag has been done, and still at the time of writing not all fifty state allow it. All that is being done is the enactment of more contro in this case how we travel. Adults can more easily discern wha makes sense and what doesn't, however kids are sponges, anc have a harder time thinking for themselves, which causes them tc be easily brainwashed. A great example for how kids are seen b the powers at hand is by a quote with uncertain origins but mos likely comes from St. Ignatius Loyola, "Give us a child till he' seven and we'll have him for life." Now look at the school systen with that light, as well as religious organizations.

THE TRANSMIGRATE MANIFESTO

Within the school system we are taught a history plagued with wrong doings and war but it is presented in a way that America is so grand and a place to take pride in, which is shown by the pledge of allegiance. Thus begins the cycle of brainwashing. When we take the pledge as kids we have no understanding of the world except that we feel safe under the flag, even if it doesn't make any sense to idolize a symbol, and the same goes for Christianity, why idolize Jesus's death when you could just as easily idolize his eternal life? As I grew older I realized how much of cult like behavior was being used with the pledge. Cults rely on a sense of safety, stability, and of course a large amount of brainwashing. When cults fail it is due to their own destructive behavior, you are seeing this take place now.

Now let me address the elephant in the room, I know there is a large veteran population that would take offense to me bashing the flag, but you too are brainwashed. You may disagree with any or all of my work the point here is to make you think, I do talk highly of some aspects but I call it how it is. This is not a new concept, I mean you were taught to run into battle not away from, which of course makes sense but it is brainwashing, yet the wars we've fought don't make the most sense. With the exception of some of the founding wars and the world wars most other wars were fought for hidden purposes. What I am about to say will start to make you question what is real, because truth is stranger than fiction, but if you stick with the material and remain conscious and contemplate what is said, true or not, it will start to remove you from the brainwashing. I do not share stories I don't believe are true or ones I don't think could've happened. I do not aim to deceive, however it is ultimately up to you what you believe is true, and beliefs create your reality.

The history of the world has its own section, however there are some points I need to make. There is a level of control on this planet that is so grand and encompassing it cannot fail unless the population wakes up from this nightmare we call life. The controllers are somehow based on an east and west basis, where the boundaries are I'm not quite certain, but it is the reasoning behind the constant east and west wars and constant fear of the west vs the east. At a more material level the biggest countries are always in war for monetary gain without much of an exception. The level of control goes as follows; These hidden controllers – Secret societies – World governments – Politicians – The people. This is a simple run down, but this is why we are not free, the people should in theory make up the entirety of this list. If we were to control the planet without the brainwashing society as we know it would crumble. There would be no wars, no us and them, no starvation, nor homelessness. If we were to take control ourselves, a sovereign people without brainwashing we would be a society of love. Think about it, what does our art and music depict? What do we all yearn for? What motivates us to do better? Love. Love can look differently for different people whether it be for another individual or its for the craft or the planet, whatever it may be it's still love. If we were to take control it would become heaven on earth but again it has to be without the constant brainwashing that is done otherwise it would be more of the same. This is what is meant in the bible a new heaven and a new earth. Yet here we stand going to our nine to fives, paying all of these taxes, thinking constantly about retirement, getting married, reproducing, maybe retiring and finally dying, all while not really being conscious of what we are doing and why we are doing them nor do we feel fulfilled for the most part. I'm not saying don't get married or don't have kids, but for so many of you barely know who your partner or kids truly are, nor do you want to be truly present parents. So many of you today give their kids technology at a young age to keep them from acting out, and to keep them out of your hair, this is not parenting this is letting the algorithm, the rectangular black mirror parent your children.

You may be thinking "what is the issue with technology?" Well think to the past, if you are younger this may not be possible, but think about how much of your life is governed by technology now. Even in the simple devices such as toasters, refrigerators, washing machines, dryers, all things now connect to the internet, the purpose really is your data, we've become a number to market to. Here's a quick story about one of the things Amazon does with data, this may be trade secret but I'll share. Amazon has people hired to write books based upon what people are searching for such as cooking recipes from mouse world or land, since there is no official cookbook out they looked into it and made their own, which even though is unofficial I've still seen it in stores. The most important technology that has come about is our media devices and computers, just think how much life has changed in the past fifteen years. How different were you? What did you do for fun? What did you do in your free time? In what ways has the work that you do changed? What was family social events and long car rides like? Think how different life is now, does it even feel like life? Or does it feel like a cheap imitation?

The Controllers gave us this technology with the intention of brainwave manipulation. As previously stated what we consume on our devices greatly impacts how we feel, and the constant consumption of these devices will literally drive you insane if you are not careful. Think of all of the mass shootings the past ten years, it is directly because of the constant psychological warfare being performed onto us, and if not them to us, it is us to us, people want to fit in and when they don't they are belittled. This is also a major reasoning to a lot of societies issues, again the insane will look upon the sane and claim they are the insane ones. Take a look at todays news if you don't believe that statement for the most part it's all negative, and if it's not negative to you it may be to someone else, what do you think that does to the psyche? My suggestion stay away from the television and your phones, not for communication but purely for the consumption of mind altering media. I can promise you this anything of importance people will let you know. Our devices are designed to keep us in a state of fear, they are meant to reinforce our egos causing us to constantly compare or judge ourselves to others, thus leading to insanity. We are seeing an increase in mentally instability and it will get worse before it gets better, my suggestion stay away from crowds in the upcoming few years, the people will rebel because they will become aware of what's going on, but until that time bad things are going to happen, and they will happen soon. Look out for building explosions that are blamed on other countries or blamed on terrorism, look out for dead presidents, look out for natural disasters (and there will be a lot of them), and most importantly look out for your own well being. The only way out of this mess is to look within and understand oneself so that you may lead by example or teach others how to know thyself.

Understand this, if you refuse to question everything, you will understand nothing, question everything and you will begin

THE TRANSMIGRATE MANIFESTO

to see the relationship between all things. This is how nature finds balance, because all is connected. Once you discover who you truly are and how you fit into the natural order of things, you will start to see how technology is impacting not only yourself and others, but how it affects all things by simple observation. Know that nature is constantly trying to grab your attention so that it may teach you this lesson but with your face in your phone or being caught up in the drama of life, it lands upon deaf ears. We are all a part of nature, there is no escaping it, you ignore, hate, or destroy it all you want but even in concrete jungles nature finds a way. It may appear in unexpected ways, if you ignore it, it may grow louder, or you may even become ill because you refuse to connect with what you are, nature. Take heed for if you constantly ignore and destroy nature, and all of the beautiful homes for the animals to roam you may just find it destroying you, whether it be literal death or rather a storm destroys your home, nature will find balance if you do not. Too often do we ignore the warning signs and spit on the sacredness of nature, be warned nature knows it is sacred because it too is conscious. Nature wishes you see it in this light because it sees you as sacred and precious in return it asks that you see it the same way. The trees and consumable plants wish nothing else but to be put to good use because they give their lives for us, you cannot even imagine how far a thank you or I love you will go when speaking to the trees or raw foods, because they are conscious they will share that love you have for them and give it right back to you. Go forth therefore blessing your food for it is holy and through the consuming of the blessed food you are blessed for are you not what you eat?

Don't miss out!

Visit the website below and you can sign up to receive emails whenever Keegan Beekman publishes a new book. There's no charge and no obligation.

https://books2read.com/r/B-A-PNZXB-XQMXD

BOOKS 2 READ

Connecting independent readers to independent writers.